Happy Birthday Sunita

Harvey Virdi

Story by Harvey Virdi and Pravesh Kumar

methuen | drama

LONDON • NEW YORK • OXFORD • NEW DELHI • SYDNEY

METHUEN DRAMA
Bloomsbury Publishing Plc
50 Bedford Square, London, WC1B 3DP, UK
1385 Broadway, New York, NY 10018, USA
29 Earlsfort Terrace, Dublin 2, Ireland

First published in Great Britain 2023

Cover design by Desk Tidy Design

A catalogue record for this book is available from the British Library.

A catalog record for this book is available from the Library of Congress.

ISBN: PB: 978-1-3504-1661-1
ePDF: 978-1-3504-1662-8
eBook: 978-1-3504-1663-5

Series: Modern Plays

Typeset by Mark Heslington Ltd, Scarborough, North Yorkshire

To find out more about our authors and books visit
www.bloomsbury.com and sign up for our newsletters.

Rifco Theatre Company in association with Watford Palace Theatre

Happy Birthday Sunita

By Harvey Virdi

Story by Harvey Virdi and Pravesh Kumar

Cast in order of appearance

Sunita	**Bhawna Baswar**
Tejpal	**Divya Seth Shah**
Harleen	**Rameet Rauli**
Nav	**Devesh Kishore**
Maurice	**Keiron Crook**

Director	Pravesh Kumar MBE
Associate Director	Ameet Chana
Designer	Colin Falconer
Dramaturg	Shelley Silas
Lighting Designer	Mark Dymock
Sound Designer	Nick Manning
Fight Director	Claire Llewellyn
Stage Management	Emma Cook & Sophie Slobodjani
Production Management	Hannah Blamire & Tom Mackey

Produced by Phoebe Cook and George Warren for Rifco Theatre Company

The original 2014 production was presented by Rifco Theatre Company and Watford Palace Theatre, and featured the following cast:

Sunita	**Clara Indrani**
Tejpal	**Shabana Azmi**
Harleen	**Goldy Notay**
Nav	**Ameet Chana**
Maurice	**Russell Floyd**

About Rifco Theatre

Artistic Director Pravesh Kumar founded Rifco Theatre Company in 2000 in Slough and it is now one of the UK's most successful touring companies. Since 2011, Rifco has been the Resident Company at Watford Palace Theatre, with a mission to inspire, entertain and inform by creating theatre of the highest quality.

Rifco develops and produces new plays and musicals, touring nationally to some of the UK's most prestigious regional theatres. They present theatre of scale and spectacle that is authentic, topical, thought-provoking, rich and entertaining and which celebrates and reflects contemporary British Asian experiences, culture and society.

Pravesh's own Indian heritage plays a fundamental role in the development of Rifco productions and his subject matter, focusing on untold stories and under-represented voices.

Rifco's success lies in understanding their audience. A vital part of creating new work is through listening and working alongside British Asian communities; Pravesh believes in gently challenging perceptions and warmly reflecting the communities he knows.

There is no other touring theatre in the country that can make this claim with new writing and provide mid-scale theatres with high-quality production values and a good box office return.

Rifco is committed to diversifying the kind of work seen in our British theatres and does this by commissioning British Asian playwrights and working with as many diverse actors, designers and directors that we can find. Rifco also provide opportunities for British Asian talent to develop their ideas and careers through our Rifco Associates programme.

Happy Birthday Sunita

Act One

Early Friday evening.

The Johal House.

Lights up on a newly renovated open-plan ground floor of a traditional terraced house.

A huge TV, a comfy leather sofa/armchair and a framed picture of Guru Nanak on the wall dominate the living room area. This lights up and twinkles when switched on.

The rest of the stage is taken up with the shiny new kitchen/diner extension, with patio doors opening onto the garden. There is a dining table and chairs, a large fridge/freezer, cooker, microwave, etc. Plates and glasses in the cupboards, a CD player/radio. A door leads to the hallway and the rest of the house. Patio doors onto the garden and garage.

A door slams.

Enter **Sunita***, in a smart office suit.*

She flings her handbag across the room. Kicks the shoes off her feet. Takes off her jacket and throws it across the room. She goes to the hall and comes back with a tatty, misshapen old cardigan. She puts it on, wrapping it around her. Then she looks around, trying to spot her handbag. When she sees it, she gets her phone out of the bag, throwing the bag aside carelessly as she falls onto the sofa. **Sunita** *checks her phone . . . there are no messages. Frustrated, she thinks for a moment, then decides to dial.*

Sunita Hello Dad. Only me, Sunita . . . just calling cos you know it's . . . so yeah, I'll see you later then. Ok. Bye.

We hear the sound of a car pulling up.

Sunita *bursts into action, putting cushions back onto the sofa, grabbing her shoes, jacket, bag, etc. as we hear the boot of the car opening and then slamming shut . . . the front door opening and slamming shut.*

Exit **Sunita** *as*

Enter **Tejpal**, *with shopping bags.*

She puts her shopping bags on the table. Takes off her coat and puts it on the back of a chair, then she opens the patio doors to let in some air. **Tejpal** *switches the Guru Nanak picture on (it twinkles brightly) and does a quick prayer. She goes to the fridge, takes a bottle of water and pours herself a glass.*

Tejpal *turns on the radio. (Mozart: Piano Concerto No 20 in D Minor.) She stands a moment, enjoying the music, her new kitchen. Then a sudden thought.*

Tejpal Sunita? Is that you? Are you home?

Beat.

She begins to prepare the party food: emptying her shopping bags, taking bowls from the cupboards and filling them with crisps, nuts, etc., placing them on the dining table. She puts plastic cups and plates on the table along with a couple of large bottles of Coke/juice, etc. happily swaying to the music as she preps the food.

Her phone pings. **Tejpal** *checks her message, it makes her smile and she starts to text back. As we hear the front door open,* **Tejpal** *quickly puts her phone away.*

Enter **Harleen** *clutching bags and bottles of prosecco. She plonks everything down.* **Tejpal** *checks* **Harleen** *hasn't damaged the table.*

Harleen Hello, Mum!

Tejpal (*Punjabi*) Hello, Harleen! Argay? (*You're here.*) How are you? Ok?

Harleen Yes, I'm ok, (*Punjabi*) thussi (*You.*) ok?

Tejpal Yes, fine.

Harleen *puts her arms around her mother-in-law; there is an awkward hug.* **Tejpal** *pats* **Harleen** *on the back.*

Tejpal Kiddha, Harleen? You've come after such a long time.

Harleen Ohhh . . . Mum! (*Punjabi*) You're looking good! (*English*) Have you had your roots done?

Tejpal Yes. You know Kamal's daughter? She did them for me.

Harleen (*impressed*) It looks nice.

Harleen *strokes* **Tejpal***'s hair.*

Tejpal Ok, Harleen, don't make it greasy.

Harleen (*broken Punjabi*) Did you go to work today?

Tejpal Yes, my god, the surgery was busy.

Harleen You don't need to go to work. (*Punjabi*) Ussi haigai. You know that don't you?

Tejpal I only do three days a week, Harleen.

Harleen You should stay at home and relax.

Tejpal Relax? (*Punjabi*) What am I going to do sitting at home all day? At least at work I have company, henna? (*Punjabi*) Shall I make some tea, Harleen?

Harleen (*Punjabi*) I don't drink tea.

Tejpal Where's Nav?

Harleen He's on his way.

Tejpal Why didn't you come together?

Harleen Mum, are you listening to classical music?

Tejpal Oh, I just put it on. (*Punjabi*) Makes a change, doesn't it?

Tejpal *turns off the radio.*

(*Punjabi*) Don't you want any tea then?

Harleen No. I don't drink tea.

Tejpal Juice?

Harleen No.

Tejpal Cola?

Harleen No.

Tejpal How was work today?

Harleen Busy. You know I'm in fashion, henna? (*Repeat in Punjabi.*)

Tejpal Yes.

Harleen So, we're doing a showcase tonight. (*Punjabi*) You know what a showcase is, Mum . . .?

Tejpal (*Punjabi*) Of course I know. (*English*) Are they showing your designs?

Harleen No. But I should really be there. I had to leave early, for Sunita's birthday.

Enter **Nav**, *adjusting his turban as he comes over to his mum for a big hug.*

Tejpal Nav! (*Punjabi*) You're here, putar!

Nav How you doing, Mum?

Tejpal Very good. (*Punjabi*) You took your time.

Nav Traffic was bad.

Tejpal Why didn't you come with Harleen?

Harleen I brought some champagne, Mum.

Nav Prosecco.

Harleen It's champagne.

Nav (*pointing out the label*) P.R.O.S.E.C.C.O. Prosecco!

Tejpal *puts out some plastic cups.*

Harleen Oh, I don't drink from plastic cups, Mum.

Tejpal Ok.

Harleen *starts to open a bottle but* **Nav** *takes the bottle off her and opens it as* **Tejpal** *gets glasses from the cupboard.*

He pours a glass. **Harleen** *puts her hand out, thinking he's pouring it out for her but he swipes it away from her and starts drinking it himself. They struggle briefly as* **Harleen** *takes the bottle from him.* **Harleen** *pours herself a glass.*

Tejpal (*Punjabi*) Eat something, you two.

Nav *begins to pick at the nibbles on the table.*

Tejpal Have a laddoo. They've come from the Baba. I asked him to bless them for you.

Nav Bless them for us? Why?

Tejpal To bring you long life and many children.

Harleen (*Punjabi*) I don't eat laddoos. (*English*) And these crisps . . . they're full of saturated fats.

Tejpal We have cake for later.

Harleen (*Punjabi*) I don't eat cake. (*English*) There's so much sugar, Mum. (*Punjabi*) It makes you 'blow-up'.

Tejpal How was your fashion show last week, Harleen?

Harleen Really good. You should've come, Mum.

Tejpal (*Punjabi*) I know, but I told you henna, (*English*) I'm busy Wednesday nights.

Nav She goes to her over 50s club, don't you Mum?

Tejpal It's good to meet people, henna?

Harleen Pour Mum some champagne.

Nav (*sarcastic*) Maybe she'd rather have a green tea? Prosecco, Mum?

Harleen (*pointed*) Champagne.

Tejpal A little one.

He pours a glass for **Tejpal**.

All Cheers!

Awkward silence . . .

Nav Where's Sunita?

Tejpal (*Punjabi*) She's not home yet.

Nav She's usually home by now, isn't she?

Harleen What are you going to do for *your* fortieth birthday, Nav?

Nav The usual. A good old-fashioned Punjabi knees-up. Hoi! Hoi! Hoi!

Harleen I want a huge party for my fortieth.

Nav Prosecco and nibbles?

Harleen And crystal chandeliers. An orchestra. Christian Dior ballgown.

Nav Sounds like *Strictly Come Dancing* to me.

Tejpal Your sister didn't want a big party. Just us. Her family.

Nav I don't think she's too fussed about being forty.

Harleen I don't think she's too fussed about anything.

Harleen *pours herself some more prosecco.*

Nav?

She holds out the bottle. There is a little 'stare-off' before **Nav** *holds out his glass for a re-fill.*

Harleen Mum?

Tejpal I've still got some.

Beat.

Tejpal Jinder's wife had the baby.

Nav I didn't even know she was pregnant.

Tejpal (*Punjabi*) I'm sure I told you. (*English*) They had a little girl. Nearly nine pounds, she was.

Nav Ouch! Not so little then!

Tejpal They named her Ruby.

Nav Ruby. Ruby. I like that name. What do you think, Harleen?

Harleen Mum, do you need some help?

Tejpal No, no, Harleen, you relax.

Nav And Harminder's had another little boy, henna?

Tejpal Yes.

Nav I saw him in ASDA last week.

Tejpal They've got three now.

Nav What did they call him?

Tejpal (*Punjabi*) I don't know. I've forgotten.

Nav Another English-sounding name?

Tejpal It's the fashion nowadays isn't it?

Harleen Did you go to the gym today, Mum?

Tejpal Yes, straight after work. I went on the running machine for half an hour.

Nav The running machine? (*Finding this funny.*) Did you *run*, Mum?

Tejpal Need to keep fit, henna.

Nav Good for you.

He gives her a hug.

Harleen I can't eat any of this, Mum. (*Picking up a packet of chocolate biscuits.*) Look, do you know what's in this?

Nav Chocolate biscuits?

Harleen Very funny. It tells you, if you read the back. Sugar. Fat. E numbers.

Tejpal I'll make you some roti.

Harleen (*Punjabi*) I don't eat roti.

Tejpal Beans on toast?

Harleen (*Punjabi*) I don't eat bread.

Tejpal What *do* you eat, Harleen?

Nav Mera sirh (*my head*)!

Tejpal How about dhal?

Harleen Did you make it with butter?

Tejpal No. Olive oil. Better for you, henna?

Harleen Oh, thank you, Mum! (*Tries to give* **Tejpal** *a hug.*) Did you hear that, Nav? Mum made dhal using olive oil!

Nav (*nasty*) Mum made dhal using olive oil?! You must be so excited!

Harleen It's a big deal actually. Mum, some more champagne?

Tejpal Why not?

Nav (*indulgent*) When did you start drinking 'prosecco', Mum?

Tejpal (*Punjabi*) Oh, you know, I tried it last year. I like it.

Tejpal *turns away to prep some food.*

Harleen *and* **Nav** *glare at each other. Beat.*

Harleen (*making sure* **Tejpal** *can't hear her*) Don't be like this.

Nav Like what?

Harleen Don't be horrible.

Nav I'm not being horrible.

Harleen What's she going to think?

Nav Why don't we ask her . . . /

Harleen Stop it!

Nav (*louder*) Mum, Harleen wants to know what . . . /

Harleen SHUSH!!

Tejpal Are you ok?

Harleen Yes.

Beat.

I need the bathroom.

Exit **Harleen.**

Tejpal (*pointedly*) Everything ok, Nav?

Nav Yeah, yeah . . .

Beat. **Tejpal** *looks at* **Nav**, *he fiddles with his turban and looks away.*

Tejpal So, what do you think of the new kitchen?

Nav Looks great, Mum. Taken a while though, hasn't it?

Tejpal (*Punjabi*) Well, nearly a year.

Nav Way too long, man. And it's over budget.

Tejpal What can you do? Covid. Brexit. The price of everything's gone up. Sometimes, Maurice didn't have enough builders to finish the job. We had to wait.

Nav You could've got a cheaper deal with some other builders.

Tejpal We would've had the same problems I think.

Nav Suppose.

Tejpal It's taken longer than we hoped but look at the quality.

Nav Yeah, the gorra's done a good job, I'll give him that. We'll see what Dad thinks later.

Awkward silence.

Has he said anything to you?

Tejpal (*Punjabi*) Who?

Nav Dad.

Beat.

Like . . . when's he coming back?

Tejpal (*Punjabi*) How do I know?

Nav I just thought . . . he might have said something to you.

Tejpal No.

Nav When he rings . . .

Tejpal When does he ring?

Mother and son stare at each other . . . so much unsaid.

Nav *fidgets with his turban.*

Nav Do you want to go to India, Mum?

Tejpal No.

Enter **Harleen**. *She picks up her glass and sips, watching, picking up the energy.*

Nav (*jolly*) We're going to India.

Harleen Are we?

Nav We're all going.

Harleen Why?

Nav For a family holiday!

Harleen Ok.

Nav Don't you want to go on holiday?

Harleen To India?

Nav I can show you the sights.

Harleen What sights?

Nav In the village?

Harleen That won't take long.

Nav You can see our farm.

Harleen I thought your dad sold the farm off to a developer?

Nav Ride through the fields on a tractor.

Harleen Isn't it a huge plastics factory now?

Nav Chew on some fresh sugar cane.

Harleen Watch the shit floating down the side of the road.

Nav It's not like that now.

Harleen You haven't been since you were ten!

Nav India's changed, man.

Harleen Can't we go to the Maldives instead?

Nav India's the next Super Power-dom!

Harleen Do you even know what that means? Anyway, I can't go.

Nav Why not?

Harleen You know why.

Harleen *and* **Nav** *eyeball each other.*

Nav So, where's the birthday girl?

Tejpal I don't know. She should be home by now.

Harleen Maybe she went for birthday drinks with her friends after work.

Nav What friends?

Harleen Don't be mean about your sister. It's her birthday.

Nav I'm not being mean, I'm just saying she hasn't got any friends.

Harleen How long has Sunita been working at the council, Mum?

Tejpal She started straight after school.

Nav So, for over twenty years, and I've never heard her mention a friend.

Harleen What does she do again?

Nav Works in the planning department. I think.

Harleen No wonder she always looks depressed.

Nav She's usually back on that sofa by half six.

Tejpal Try her mobile, Nav.

Nav *rings.* **Harleen** *starts to empty her bags.*

Harleen (*broken Punjabi*) I brought some decorations, Mum.

Tejpal (*worried*) She should be back by now.

Harleen I thought we'd put up some birthday decorations . . .

Nav It's gone straight to voicemail.

Harleen Maybe it'll cheer her up.

Nav She must have it switched off.

Harleen She's gone for a birthday drink. About time she had some fun.

Tejpal She didn't tell me she was going out.

Harleen (*throwing* **Nav** *some balloons*) You can make a start on these.

Tejpal She usually tells me if she is going to be late.

Nav When is she ever late?

Harleen They probably surprised her at work.

Nav She'll be home soon, Mum, don't worry about it.

Tejpal (*Punjabi*) Call her office.

Nav There won't be anyone in the office now, will there?

Harleen It's gone six.

Tejpal Something must have happened. (*Punjabi*) Nav, call the hospital.

Nav We don't need to call the hospital!

Tejpal She should be home by now.

Nav Mum, it's her birthday. She's allowed to go out for a drink. Just chill!

Beat.

She'll be back before Dad calls.

Harleen *and* **Tejpal** *share a look. Silence.*

Harleen Nav? Balloons *please*!

Nav *begins to blow up balloons.*

Harleen Look, Mum, I brought a banner. Do you like it?

She shows off the 'happy 40th birthday' banner.

Tejpal Did you bring blue-tack?

Harleen No, but I have sellotape.

Tejpal I don't want sellotape marks on my new kitchen walls.

Harleen Oh.

Nav Blu-tack leaves marks too, Mum. You should've put the decorations up last night.

Harleen It's supposed to be a surprise.

Nav Yeah?

Harleen So she would've seen them this morning wouldn't she? Buddhoo (*fool*).

Nav Oi!

Harleen Where do you want me to put the banner, Mum? (*Holding it against a pristine wall.*) Here?

Tejpal No, no! Just leave everything there. I'll do it.

As **Tejpal** *turns away,* **Nav** *grabs* **Harleen***'s hand and pulls her towards him. He pretends to head-butt* **Harleen** *with his turban. This eventually makes* **Harleen** *smile. She goes in for a cheeky kiss,* **Nav** *doesn't want his mother to catch them but they have a quick kiss/cuddle.* **Nav** *pulls away as* **Tejpal** *turns back.*

Tejpal Harleen?

Harleen Hunji? (*As she smacks* **Nav***'s bottom.*)

Tejpal (*handing her some plates*) Put these on the table. And put the cake in the middle.

Harleen *looks around for the cake.*

Harleen Where's the cake, Mum?

Tejpal What?

Harleen The cake? Did you hide it in the garage?

Tejpal You were going to pick up the cake.

Harleen Us? When?

Tejpal (*annoyed*) I ordered an eggless cake last Monday and all week I've been telling you to remember to pick it up for today.

Harleen You didn't tell *me*, Mum!

Tejpal (*Punjabi*) How can I tell you? (*English*) I never see you. Nav comes round every day . . .

Harleen (*under her breath*) Of course he does.

Tejpal I asked him to pick up the cake.

Nav I'll go and get it now.

Tejpal It's too late now. The shop closed at six.

Harleen (*to* **Nav**) You could have told me about the cake. Now it's my fault we haven't got one.

Harleen *pours herself more prosecco, she is slowly getting drunk.*

Nav Nobody's saying it's your fault!

Harleen Your mum's blaming me.

Nav No she isn't.

Harleen Yes she is! Look at her! She's all hunched up. Even her shoulders are glaring at me!

Nav (*laughing*) Shut up. You're such a drama queen.

Enter **Sunita**, *in her pyjamas and the tatty old cardi.*

Harleen Now there's another reason for her to hate me . . .

Nav Mum doesn't hate you, Harleen . . .

Harleen I just get everything thrown back in my face . . .

Throughout the following, **Sunita** *makes herself a cup of tea . . . as she waits for the kettle to boil, she listens to what they are saying about her, but they are so wrapped up in their bickering, they pay no attention to her.*

Harleen I brought balloons and party poppers . . .

Nav It's ok . . .

Harleen I wanted to make it really nice for your sister . . .

Nav We'll work something out.

Harleen Not that she appreciates anything I do for her either . . .

Nav She didn't even want a party.

Harleen Look at these beautiful candles. I had them specially made. Where are we going to put the candles if we don't have a birthday cake?

Nav I bet you she won't even notice.

Harleen That's not the point. I know your sister mopes around all day pretending she doesn't care about anything . . .

Nav She's just grumpy sometimes.

Harleen And I know she said she didn't want a party . . .

Tejpal I told her to invite some friends over tonight. She said no.

Nav That's because she hasn't got any friends!

Harleen But we can't ignore her birthday. It's her fortieth!

Nav We'll go to Tesco and get her another cake.

Tejpal I ordered a special eggless birthday cake from Ravinder's Bakery.

Nav Why does it have to be an eggless? We're not even vegetarians!

Tejpal They taste nicer.

Harleen She's obviously having some kind of breakdown.

Nav Don't be stupid.

Harleen Think about it. She's forty. She's single and she's still living at home with her mum.

Nav You think she's having a mid-life crisis?

Harleen, *who's been drinking throughout, is now getting a little hyper.*

Harleen Nav, we need a cake for your sister's fortieth birthday!

Nav Don't you think I know that!

Harleen Why didn't you tell me?! You should've told me.

Nav I did, actually! But you were too busy getting ready for another one of your reception drinks shit, so you weren't listening, as usual.

Harleen Do you mind? I'm in fashion. And people, important people who work in fashion, come to these events.

Sunita I am in the room you know. And I'm not deaf.

Shocked silence. Eventually . . .

Harleen Happy Birthday, Sunita!

Exit **Sunita**, *taking her tea with her.*

Nav (*to Mum*) I thought you said she wasn't home yet?

Tejpal She must have come back early.

Harleen Do you think she heard us?

Nav Well, let's put it like this, Harleen, I don't think we need to worry about a birthday cake now do we?

Tejpal Shut up, both of you! As usual, if I want something done, I have to do it myself. Harleen, make the atta. We need to make roti. Nav, do the salad. I'll phone my friend. We can't do a birthday party without a cake.

Tejpal *takes her phone and exits.*

They work in silence . . . **Nav** *takes salad stuff from the fridge . . . a chopping board and a knife, a bowl, etc. . . . He starts chopping.* **Harleen** *studies the bag of atta (chapatti flour), trying to read the instructions . . .*

Harleen (*pathetically*) I don't know how to guhn the atta.

Nav For God's sake, Harleen.

Beat. Then, flirty, she puts her arm round him and kisses him. **Nav**, *still annoyed, pushes her advances away.*

Harleen Don't be like that.

Nav Stop it, Harleen.

Harleen (*flirty*) Nav . . .?

Nav Tch!

Harleen God, you're the grumpy one sometimes!

Nav Harleen!

Harleen What?

Nav DON'T!

She dumps the bag of atta in front of him.

Nav *continues chopping while* **Harleen** *sips her prosecco and eats crisps.*

Silence.

Harleen I wonder how long she's been hiding upstairs.

Nav Who knows?

Harleen It's . . . creepy.

Nav When we have kids, there's no way I'm going to let them sit in their room all day, doing nothing.

Harleen She's your sister.

Nav So?

Harleen Do something.

Nav Like what?

Harleen It's not right.

Nav She's always been like that.

Harleen Nav, we're a modern family.

Nav And?

Harleen And it's ok if your sister's a lesbian.

Nav She's not a bloody lesbian!

Harleen Of course she's a lesbian!

Nav Oh so now you're the expert are you?

Harleen It's pretty obvious! That's the reason why she's always looking so pissed off. She's lonely. I can introduce her to some colleagues. I have gay friends.

Nav So, two women can get married in the Gurdwara now?

Harleen I'm trying to help here. Your sister is depressed and you're all pretending it's perfectly normal.

Nav (*losing it*) She's not depressed, all right!

Harleen All right! I'm just saying she looks it.

Nav She can't help how she looks, can she?

Harleen Fine.

Nav Fine.

Silence. **Nav** *chops,* **Harleen** *drinks.*

Harleen It's Friday.

Nav I know it's Friday, Harleen.

Harleen So *is* your dad calling tonight do you think?

Silence.

Harleen *takes a gulp of prosecco and some crisps . . .* **Nav** *looks at her, then the crisps she's been stuffing herself with.*

Nav (*mimics her, in Punjabi*) I don't eat crisps.

Harleen *pushes the crisps away from her. She watches* **Nav**.

Beat.

Harleen He's been gone a long time, hasn't he?

Nav Who?

Harleen Your dad.

Nav Yeah.

Harleen He's not coming back, is he?

Nav He will.

Harleen Yeah?

Nav Of course.

Harleen Have you asked him?

Nav Don't need to ask him, do I?

Harleen He loves being in India, doesn't he?

Nav I guess . . .

Harleen He's got his big house, his big car and his new . . .

Nav I think you've had a bit too much 'champagne'.

Harleen He's getting on with his life.

Nav Shut up, Harleen.

Harleen I'm just saying! Everyone's thinking it. So why can't you . . .

Nav Why can't I what?

Harleen Come on, Nav! Just for once, we can go out on a Friday night. Go into town, have dinner, see friends . . . instead of sitting around waiting for him to call. And he never does, does he? (*To herself.*) I don't know who he thinks he is.

Nav (*suddenly vulnerable*) He's my dad, Harleen. I know he's . . . but . . . he's my dad.

Harleen *takes* **Nav** *in her arms and holds him. There is a moment of tenderness.*

Enter **Tejpal**. **Nav** *pulls away from* **Harleen**.

Tejpal Lovely jubbly.

Nav What was that?

Nav *and* **Harleen** *share an amused look.*

Nav Lovely jubbly . . .? Mum's learning cockney slang! Apples and pears! Apples and pears! Would you Adam and Eve it!

Tejpal Shut up. My friend's bringing the cake.

Harleen I thought this was just going to be a quiet family thing?!

She takes a mirror from her handbag and checks her make-up.

Nav Your friend's going to get hold of a cake . . .

Harleen Eggless cake.

Nav Eggless cake at this time of night?

Tejpal (*sharply*) I've sorted it!!

Silence. **Harleen** *sips her prosecco.*

Harleen Sorry, Mum, about you know, forgetting the cake. Nav forgot to tell me, didn't you, Nav? We're both really sorry. Aren't we, Nav?

Nav (*glaring at* **Harleen**) Yeah, sorry, Mum.

Harleen *tries to hug her mother-in-law.* **Tejpal** *pats her on the back.*

Tejpal (*Punjabi*) Doesn't matter now, Harleen. (*English*) It's ok.

Harleen But I would have remembered to pick it up if you'd told *me*.

Tejpal Harleen, eat something.

Harleen I don't feel like eating, Mum. I haven't got an appetite.

Nav (*vindictive*) Sure you're not pregnant?

Harleen *glares at* **Nav** *who looks at her challengingly . . . As an overjoyed* **Tejpal** *starts to fuss over* **Harleen**.

Tejpal Kee? Harleen, are you pregnant? Nav? Suchi? Oh my God, this is happy news!

Tejpal *does a quick thank you to the twinkling picture of Guru Nanak.*

(*Punjabi*) Such happy news! (*English*) Come and sit. Sit here. Come.

Tejpal *tries to take the glass out of* **Harleen**'*s hand . . . there is a struggle but* **Tejpal** *wins.*

Tejpal You mustn't drink anymore. Ok? This is wonderful news. I'm so happy. So happy!

Harleen (*to* **Nav**) You're raising her hopes. Stop it.

Tejpal Today is a double celebration!!!

Nav Mum.

Tejpal You have to take it easy ok, Harleen?

Nav MUM!

Tejpal Ke?

Beat.

Nav Harleen's not pregnant. We were joking.

Tejpal Joking?

Harleen I'm not pregnant.

Tejpal *is bewildered.*

Harleen Sorry.

Nav Sorry.

Tejpal You think this is funny? You think you can treat me like an idiot?

Nav No, of course not.

Tejpal You think I'm stupid?

Harleen No . . .

Nav She said sorry. She didn't mean it.

Harleen *We* didn't mean it!

Harleen *gives* **Tejpal** *a hug.*

Harleen Sorry, Mum.

Silence.

Mum, look what I brought for Sunita. (*Looking for the present.*) Where is it? Nav, where's Sunita's present?

Nav I don't know.

Harleen I told you to put it in your car.

Nav Was that before or after you slammed the door in my face?

Harleen You'll have to go home and get it.

Nav Mum's making roti!

Harleen It's down the road!

Nav You go and get it.

Harleen (*hysterical*) It's your sister's fortieth birthday Nav!

Nav For god's sake, Harleen, calm down! You're doing my head in.

Exit **Nav**, *grabbing his keys off the table and grumbling under his breath.*

Harleen And hurry up. It'll be time to cut the cake soon!

Nav (*off*) We don't even have a bloody cake yet!

The door slams. Silence.

Harleen *pulls herself together . . .*

Harleen I've got a scarf for Sunita.

Tejpal That's nice.

Harleen And I put some money in the birthday card.

Tejpal How much did you put in?

Harleen Nav wanted to put £51. But I said we should put £101.

Tejpal I'll write that down, so I won't forget.

Harleen I hope she likes it. I designed it especially for her.

Tejpal I'm sure she will, Harleen.

Harleen I'm sure she won't. You know what she's like. Mum, you should wear your scarf like they do in Paris. It's the fashion nowadays.

She starts to tie **Tejpal***'s chunni in a fancy bow over the following conversation. It is awkward.*

Tejpal So, your work is going well, Harleen?

Harleen Oh yes. You know I'm in fashion, henna?

Tejpal Yes, you've told me.

Harleen Well, I had a meeting last week.

Tejpal Really?

Harleen Do you know Gok Wan?

Tejpal Oh yes, he's on the TV, henna?

Harleen Well, it wasn't him. It was with someone who knows him. So, you know, fingers crossed.

Tejpal Ok . . .

Harleen And I'm organizing another fashion show. And this time, they might let me show my designs. Afterwards, there will be champagne and cheesy nibbles. You must come this time.

Tejpal I will.

Harleen Promise?

Tejpal Promise.

Harleen My Punjabi's getting better, henna? Don't you think?

Tejpal Yes, it's very good.

Harleen Nav's been teaching me.

Tejpal Well done, Harleen.

Harleen Mum?! You're wearing lipstick?

Tejpal I always used to, when I first got married but then when . . . There was a special offer in John Lewis. The lady said it suited me.

Harleen Mmm . . . It's a bit *pink*.

Tejpal Hurry up, Harleen, I need to make roti.

Harleen I've nearly finished.

Tejpal Don't make it too tight.

Harleen You have to suffer for fashion, Mum!

Tejpal Is that why you don't eat anything?

Harleen No, Mum . . . The thing is, I've got loads of allergies, henna? I'm lactose intolerant, wheat intolerant, if I eat, I get bloated. I blow up.

Tejpal Put the tava on the cooker please, Harleen.

Harleen You making roti in here, Mum?

Tejpal (*proud*) I'm using my new kitchen for the first time today.

Harleen But the house will smell! Why are you using your new kitchen when you went to all the trouble of fitting the old one in the garage? Doesn't make any sense. Look how beautiful and new this one is, keep it as your show kitchen like everyone else.

Tejpal I want to enjoy it, not show off with it. Life's too bloody short!

Harleen (*shocked*) Are you ok, Mum?

Tejpal Yes of course. Why?

Harleen Umm . . . nothing.

Harleen *puts the tava on the cooker . . .*

Tejpal Wait! Let me do the blessing first.

Harleen *holds the tava while* **Tejpal** *unties her chunni (undoing* **Harleen**'*s fancy bow) and covers her head, she says a quick prayer over the cooker.*

Tejpal Now put it on.

Harleen How does the cooker work, Mum?

Tejpal (*exasperated*) Just turn the knob, Harleen. And get a fresh tea towel from the drawer.

Harleen It's not very hygienic, henna, using a tea towel?

Tejpal It's clean, (*Punjabi*) nothing will happen to you. Where's the atta, Harleen?

Harleen Oh. Um. Nav didn't guhn the atta. I said I'd do it but he wouldn't let me. Do you want me to do it now?

Tejpal Just leave it. I have some ready made roti in the freezer.

Tejpal *gets busy getting the roti from the freezer, getting her tea towel ready, etc.*

Harleen Nav puts so much butter on his roti, I keep telling him, it's the quickest route to blocked arteries. But he won't listen to me.

Tejpal I hardly use any butter nowadays.

Harleen That's so good, Mum.

Tejpal I use olive oil for everything.

Harleen You can use coconut oil as well.

Tejpal And I only make allo parathas twice a week.

Harleen But you should try to have no parathas.

Tejpal Have to keep tabs on the cholesterol, henna?

Harleen You know what cholesterol is, Mum?

Tejpal Of course I know! I'm not stupid you know.

Beat.

Harleen Have you tried wheat-free atta?

Tejpal No.

Harleen I'll bring some for you.

Tejpal (*not convinced*) Oh. Ok.

Harleen More champagne?

Tejpal Why not?

Harleen *tops up their glasses.*

Both Cheers!

Tejpal My god, the tava isn't hot. I told you to put the cooker on.

Harleen I did.

Tejpal Turn the heat up.

Harleen There's something wrong with the cooker.

Harleen *starts pressing all the different knobs and buttons.*

Tejpal (*protective*) Just leave it, Harleen.

Enter **Sunita**.

Harleen (*Punjabi*) Happy Birthday, Sunita.

Sunita *ignores her.* **Harleen** *is embarrassed at her attempt to say 'Happy Birthday' in Punjabi.*

Harleen Hope you've had a good day.

Tejpal You came home early?

Sunita Yes.

Tejpal Are you all right?

Sunita (*grumpy*) Yes.

Tejpal We'll be eating birthday dinner soon.

Sunita *is opening and slamming shut cupboard doors.*

Tejpal (*Punjabi, to* **Harleen**) You know Mindo's mother? (*English*) She had another heart attack.

Harleen Oh really?

Tejpal We all have to go one day.

Harleen Hmm.

Tejpal (*Punjabi*) God writes your kismet on the day you are born.

Harleen Hmm . . .

Tejpal Only he knows how long we will be on this earth.

Harleen I don't know if I believe that . . .

Sunita *slamming shut another cupboard door.*

Tejpal Sunita, mind my new cupboards please.

Sunita I can't find the Nutella.

Harleen Did you know, there's four times more sugar in a jar of Nutella than a bottle of Coke?

Sunita *slams another cupboard door.*

Tejpal (*Punjabi*) Look in the fridge.

Sunita What's it doing in the fridge? It'll be all hard now. God! Nothing's where it should be!

Tejpal Well the kitchen's finished now. You can put it back in the cupboard.

Sunita Thank god.

Tejpal Everything's been signed off.

Sunita About bloody time! Don't know why you wanted a new kitchen. The old one was fine.

Awkward silence as **Sunita** *makes herself a Nutella sandwich.*

Tejpal (*Punjabi*) How was work today, Sunita?

Sunita Fine.

Tejpal You came home early?

Sunita God, what is this? Hundred questions?

Harleen You never come home early.

Sunita So all right, Miss Marple, I came home early. I didn't know I had to let the world and his wife know!

Tejpal (*Punjabi*) We're only asking, Sunita. (*English*) You don't have to be like that.

Sunita (*hiding her upset*) I just . . . I wanted to come home, all right?

Harleen *and* **Tejpal** *share a look.*

Harleen (*kind*) I bet they did a surprise birthday cake for you at work!

Sunita No.

Harleen Cards?

Sunita No.

Harleen They must have sung Happy Birthday?!

Sunita No.

Harleen Oh.

Sunita *pours herself a glass of milk and sits down to eat her sandwich.*

Tejpal (*Punjabi*) Harleen, you know Vimla? (*English*) Her husband runs the off-licence on Woodley Road?

Harleen Um . . . I don't think so.

Tejpal Yes you do. She came to your wedding. Brought the lime green sari with the red sequins?

Harleen Oh yes, the hideous sari that gets passed around every year?

Tejpal Her son-in-law died. Can you believe? Only been married four years.

Harleen That's terrible.

Tejpal Heart attack. He was only forty-two.

Harleen Hmm.

Tejpal You don't know what's going to happen in life, henna?

Harleen You do if you have six parathas, four cans of Stella and a laddoo for breakfast every morning.

Tejpal True.

Beat.

So, Harleen, you and Nav must've talked about having a family, henna?

Harleen We've talked about it.

Tejpal You've been married how long?

Harleen I don't think how long, because, when you're happy, you don't need to, do you?

Sunita Ten years two months next week isn't it?

Harleen Is it?

Tejpal You want a family don't you, Harleen?

Harleen Yeah, of course we do. Not just yet. I'm so busy at work. I need to build up my business. Have at least one collection out before we think about all that.

Tejpal Harleen, work comes and goes. Life is always busy. Don't let it get in the way of family. Don't leave it too late, ok bete?

Beat.

Harleen What are you wearing for your party, Sunita? Going to dress up later?

Sunita No.

Harleen But it's your fortieth!

Sunita You don't have to keep harping on about it!

Harleen That's a nice cardigan, is it vintage?

Sunita It's my dad's actually.

Harleen (*under her breath*) Looks like it could do with a wash.

Sunita Don't order me around like you do my brother.

Harleen I don't need to order Nav around. He has a mind of his own.

Sunita Right! He can't do a thing without your say-so.

Harleen Why are you so mean?

Sunita I just don't like you.

Tejpal Sunita! Stop that.

Harleen I don't know why you're so . . . so . . . I don't know why I bother.

Tejpal (*Punjabi*) Why are you eating that?

Sunita I'm starving.

Tejpal We're having your birthday dinner soon.

Sunita We can't. We have to wait for Dad.

Harleen (*under her breath*) Oh for god's sake, not this again.

Sunita What did you say?

Harleen Nothing. Where's Nav? I could have walked there and back by now.

Sunita Then why didn't you? Oh yeah, I just remembered, you like bossing my brother around.

Tejpal Sunita . . .

Sunita What?

Tejpal Chup.

Sunita God! Can't even have an opinion now!

Sunita *eats crisps . . . loudly.*

Harleen (*to* **Sunita**) I brought some champagne. Do you want some? Mum's had a glass.

Sunita *checks her phone.*

Sunita Since when has Mum been drinking champagne?

Tejpal Sunita, stop playing with your phone and get the dhal from the fridge.

Sunita (*going to her mum*) Champagne, Mum? Since when?

Tejpal (*Punjabi*) Can't I have a glass? (*English*) To celebrate my beautiful daughter's special birthday?

Suddenly, **Sunita** *gives her mum a fierce hug.*

Beat.

Harleen, *feeling left out, goes to them . . . a moment of solidarity.*

Harleen I don't like using microwaves, the x-rays kill off all the goodness.

Sunita Electromagnetic radiation actually. Non-ionizing radiation, you know, the same as your phone or the radio. Stuff like that. Don't look so surprised. I'm not stupid.

Harleen I didn't say . . .

Sunita I was on the fast track to Oxbridge.

Harleen Nav didn't tell me. I thought you hated school.

Sunita I had a place at Imperial College to do physics. Do you remember, Mum, when my letter came, saying I'd got in? I screamed so loud, Nav dropped his sugar puffs all over the kitchen floor.

Harleen But why didn't you go?

Sunita (*pointedly*) Ask Mum.

Harleen You should've gone. It opened my eyes, to new experiences, new people. It totally changed the way I view the world.

Sunita (*sarcastic*) Well lucky you.

Harleen I'm just saying.

Silence.

Sunita You *are* lucky. Look at you . . . You don't even know it.

Harleen I count my blessings every day actually.

Sunita Good for you. Got a Gratitude Journal have you?

Harleen It's part of my daily practice . . .

Sunita I don't have any blessings to count. I wasn't allowed to have any, was I, Mum?

Tejpal Don't be silly, Sunita.

Sunita Oh, so now I'm silly.

Harleen What do you mean?

Beat.

Tejpal Things were different then.

Sunita (*sarcastic, resentment*) Oh yeah, I forgot. Things were different then. Then, you had to be 'good', didn't you Mum? No going out. No after-school clubs. And if you were clever, tough shit. After all, making roti and washing your husband's chuddies is a higher art form. Who needs to understand calculus or geometry to do that?

Tejpal Those times have gone.

Sunita Have they? Have they really?

Harleen My mummy and daddy, they wanted me to get an education.

Sunita *Lucky* you . . .

Tejpal Sunita . . .

Sunita My parents wanted me to toe the party line. 'What will people say? What will they think?' Keep your head down and don't give anyone a chance to gossip about you.

Tejpal I never said that.

Sunita YES YOU DID. You were so busy trying to keep your head down, you didn't see what it was doing to me. So yes, Harleen, in answer to your earlier questions, when you thought I wasn't here, I'm forty, I'm single and I'm still living at home with my mum. That's right. Lucky lucky me!

Nav went skipping off to university, not in a care in the world, drinking and farting his way through some dodgy Media Studies degree. But I'm the one with the brain cells. I should've gone to university. Nav's as thick as pig shit.

Harleen Oi, that's my husband you're talking about!

Sunita Well, he might have fooled you, but I know he's thick. (*The front door slams.*) Talk of the devil . . .

Enter **Nav**, *with a beautifully wrapped present, which he gives to* **Harleen**.

He fidgets with his turban.

Harleen You took your time!

She tries to give him a cuddle.

Nav I wasn't even gone ten minutes!

Sunita We're waiting for Dad before we eat.

There is an awkward look between **Tejpal**, **Nav** *and* **Harleen**.

Nav What were you doing upstairs all that time, sis?

Sunita Nothing much.

Nav Why you sitting around on your own for? You should have come down. It's your birthday.

He goes over to the CD player and pops in a CD.

Look what I got! It's my sister's fortieth birthday, man! It's time for some Hoi! Hoi! Hoi!

'Gidha Pao' (djVix, Miss Pooja) starts . . . He starts dancing.

We need to get this party started! Come on, Sunita, dance! Let me see you throw some classic Punjabi shapes!

Sunita No thanks.

Nav Come on!

Sunita Get off me!

Nav Dance with me.

Sunita I don't want to!

Nav (*dancing around her*) Hoi! Hoi! Hoi!

Sunita Stop it! I don't like it.

Nav What you talking about? (*Mimicking her.*) I don't like it! I bet you can't remember some of our old routines?

Sunita Yeah, well, we were kids! It was stupid.

Tejpal They would do a show for us every Sunday afternoon.

Harleen Really? That's so sweet, Nav.

Nav We'd spend all week coming up with a new routine.

Sunita Excuse me, I was the choreographer, I spent all week coming up with a new routine!

Nav True. But it was my job to get hold of the latest bhangra tunes. No Spotify or Apple to download whatever you wanted. I spent all my time . . .

Tejpal And money . . .

Nav In the Indian record shops.

Sunita I had to sort out the costumes. You should have seen him on the sewing machine.

Nav Come on! I gave it a go. Just couldn't get the hang of it!

Sunita See? (*Smiling, despite herself.*) Thick as pig shit . . .

Sunita *starts to dance with her brother.* **Tejpal** *and* **Harleen** *get pulled in – they dance, lost in their family moment, happy.*

We hear loud knocking on the front door. The family are too engrossed in their dancing to hear it.

Another loud knock on the door. **Sunita** *hears the knocking and stops dancing. The others are still having a good time.*

Another loud knocking

Sunita It's Dad!

Nav Dad?

Sunita He's come for my birthday! I knew he'd come. I knew he'd be here!!

Sunita *runs off to answer the door.*

Tejpal, **Nav** *and* **Harleen** *are speechless.* **Nav** *turns the music off. They wait, uncomfortable.*

Enter **Maurice**, *holding a cake box, a beautiful bunch of flowers and blue-tack. Followed by* **Sunita**.

Maurice What's all this then? You started the party without me!

End of Act One.

Act Two

Sunita *is curled up on the sofa, upset, her dad's old cardi wrapped around her, checking her phone.*

Tejpal How are you, Maurice?

Maurice Good. Good.

Harleen *and* **Nav** *are surprised.*

Tejpal You all know Maurice.

Nav Yeah . . .

Maurice All right mate?

They shake hands.

Maurice Where's the birthday girl?

Harleen On the sofa.

Maurice Right.

He gives **Sunita** *the flowers.*

Maurice Happy birthday, Sunita.

Beat.

Tejpal They're beautiful. Say thank you Maurice.

Sunita Thank you, Maurice.

Maurice You're welcome, Sunita.

He gives her a gentle pat on the back, **Sunita** *hides herself away on the sofa.*

Silence. Awkward.

Nav Sorry, um . . . what are you doing here? Is it something to do with the kitchen? Can't it wait till Monday?

Harleen The cooker's not working.

Maurice Your mum invited me. Sunita's birthday . . .?

Nav Oh. Right.

Harleen We can't get the cooker to work.

Tejpal Thanks for picking up the birthday cake, Maurice.

Maurice No problem. Can't celebrate the big four-O without a cake can we? And here's the blue-tack.

Nav Mum's being precious about her new walls.

Harleen I haven't even put up the birthday decorations yet, she wouldn't let me use sellotape.

Maurice Quite right. Sellotape ruins the paint work.

Tejpal *takes the cake out of the box and puts a big '40' candle in it.* **Nav** *and* **Harleen** *share a confused look.*

Maurice You started without me then?

Nav Nah, that was just a bit of . . .

Maurice Bhangra. I could hear it blaring outside. No wonder you didn't hear me knocking.

Nav I found some old CDs.

Maurice Nice. Love a bit of bhangra.

Harleen You've heard of bhangra?

Maurice I was quite into it, back in the day.

Nav Yeah?

Maurice Yeah, I was part of a bhangra group back in the 80s. Did a bit of drumming on them dhols, you know? Went up and down the country for weddings and whatnots. Loved it. We had a laugh, me and the boys . . . yeah . . . Those were the days. Do you know Nikka Baba?

Nav Never heard of him.

Maurice He was best man at my wedding. Lives in Leicester now. He got me into it. He started this bhangra group and needed a couple of dhol drummers. I used to play the drums at school, that's how we met . . . and it just took off. He had a great voice. Tell you what, it's a good workout isn't it? (*Laughing – he does some classic bhangra moves.*) My knees can't take it these days, do know what I mean?

They stare at him. **Nav** *has a little fidget with his turban . . .*

There is an awkward silence.

Nav Didn't recognize you for a minute!

Maurice I'm not in me overalls.

Harleen Nice coat, Maurice.

Maurice Thanks, I like it. You must be Harleen?

Harleen It's Armani isn't it?

Maurice Got it in Milan last year. I hear you're in fashion?

Harleen That's right.

Maurice Keeping you busy?

Harleen Really busy actually. I'm working on a new collection at the moment.

Maurice Good for you. Won't be long before we see your designs in one of them posh magazines.

Harleen I hope so. (*She looks at* **Nav**, *pointedly.*)

Let me take your coat, Maurice.

Maurice Thanks, Harleen.

Harleen I'll even put it on a hanger.

Exit **Harleen** *with his coat.*

Nav Mum asked you to get the cake?

Maurice Yeah, she asked me if I could pick it up on my way over. It was no bother. I drive right past the shop.

Nav I thought it closed at six.

Maurice It does. I gave Ravinder a quick call, told him I'd be passing by. He was happy to do a friend a favour.

Nav Right.

Maurice He had a double extension done, just before Covid. He's a good man. Do you know him?

Nav Nah.

Beat.

Maurice Your lot like your extensions, don't you?

Nav Cheaper than moving I suppose.

Maurice Suppose.

Enter **Harleen**.

Tejpal Nav, get Maurice a drink.

Harleen We got champagne.

Nav It's prosecco.

Tejpal Maybe Maurice would like a beer.

Nav I didn't get any beers in, Mum.

Tejpal There's beer in the fridge.

Nav (*confused*) You bought beer?

Tejpal For the party.

Sunita (*still sitting on the sofa*) I didn't want a party.

Maurice I wouldn't say no to a nice glass of bubbly.

Harleen Try this . . . (*she pours him a glass*) it's a gold medal winner from Waitrose!

Maurice Lovely.

Harleen *hands him a glass and tops up everyone else.*

Beat . . . they look at each other, uncertain . . .

Maurice To the birthday girl! Cheers!

Harleen (*loudly*) Cheers!

They clink glasses. **Sunita** *and* **Nav** *glare at* **Harleen***, she tries to hide her discomfort but* **Maurice** *seems oblivious.*

Harleen Cheesy puffs, Maurice?

Maurice Thanks, Harleen, don't mind if I do.

Harleen *and* **Maurice** *chat as . . .*

Nav (*Punjabi*) Mum, what's he doing here?

Tejpal There's nothing wrong with inviting friends over.

Sunita (*in bad Punjabi*) He's not my friend.

Tejpal He knew it was your birthday today.

Sunita How?

Nav We're stuck with him now.

Sunita I don't want him here.

Tejpal Sunita, chup. Help me with the table.

During the following **Sunita** *and* **Tejpal** *prepare the rest of the food, getting bowls and dishes from the microwave, putting plates on the table, etc.*

Nav Thanks, mate, for bringing the cake.

Maurice My pleasure.

Nav Harleen and I, we completely forgot to pick it up.

Harleen I knew nothing about it. He didn't tell me.

Maurice It happens.

Nav I should have remembered, it was the only thing Mum asked me to do.

Maurice What do you think of the extension?

Nav You done a good job.

Maurice I got a good team.

Nav You were supposed to be done months ago. And it's over budget.

Maurice The devil's in the detail. Covid's not helped. And don't get me started on the Brexit fiasco. Trying to get hold of materials – nightmare! The price of everything going through the roof. And a lot of my good men moved away. There's been a lot of juggling, let me tell you. Everyone's in the same boat.

Nav Yeah.

Maurice I'm pleased with how it's turned out. But more importantly, your mum's happy. Do you know Harish Kaka at H.E.P Supplies?

Nav No.

Maurice Oh, he's a good man. He sorted me out with this great kit.

Nav Yeah?

Maurice Your mum had me put the old kitchen in the garage.

Nav All the real cooking gets done in the garage nowadays.

Harleen We don't want the house to smell.

Maurice Funny that isn't? When I was a boy, we'd say, hello, the Indians next door are cooking something dodgy again. And now, curry's our national dish. We love it and you're trying to hide it!

Nav Is there anything outstanding? Do I need to settle up with you?

Maurice No, no, we're sorted.

Harleen The cooker isn't working.

Maurice Tej, I was just telling Nav, we're all sorted.

Sunita Tej?

Nav, **Sunita** *and* **Harleen** *share a quiet look.*

Tejpal Yes.

Nav What about the cooker?

Harleen It isn't working.

Maurice I'll take a look. It was fine. I double-checked everything myself.

Maurice *rolls up his sleeves and moving* **Nav** *and* **Harleen** *out of the way he starts to fiddle with the cooker.*

Harleen *tops up their glasses.* **Nav** *and* **Harleen** *share a look. They sip their drinks . . . eat a few crisps . . .*

Nav So, Maurice, what's next for you? Got another extension?

Maurice I'm having a break.

Harleen Holiday?

Tejpal Maurice is semi-retired, he lives in Spain.

Harleen Really?

Maurice Got a place just outside Marbella.

Nav Nice.

Maurice I only come over to give my brother a hand. Kitchens. Extensions. You name it, we build it. East End boys done good.

Harleen Oh, I love the East End. Spitalfields, Brick Lane, Columbia Road flower market.

Maurice That's where we grew up. Wasn't trendy like it is now.

Nav The National Front were big round there back in the day.

Maurice Yeah, that's right.

Nav Local skinheads ganging up on the brown people. Couldn't walk down the street without getting your head kicked in.

Maurice It weren't good. People said and did some bad things.

Nav People died. You must've been part of all that?

Maurice Couldn't miss it if it was happening down your street. The hard thing was trying to keep out of it.

Nav And did you? Keep out of it?

Maurice I did my best. The cooker's fine. You just hadn't switched it on at the socket, Harleen.

Harleen Oh. Can I pick your brains, Maurice? I've been telling Nav for ages. We should invest in property. Buy somewhere cheap, get the builders in to do it up, then rent it out.

Nav She's obsessed with *Homes Under the Hammer*.

Harleen Nav thinks I'm mad but we could easily build up a little property portfolio.

Maurice Can't go wrong with bricks and mortar.

Harleen That's what I said! Maybe you can come in with us as our builder? We can be a team.

Maurice I'm heading back to Spain, Harleen.

Harleen I've got a great eye for colour and interior design. You can do all the structural changes and . . .

Maurice I can put you in touch with my brother if you like.

Nav You need money to start doing that sort of thing.

Harleen Daddy can lend us the money. He's already offered. (*To* **Maurice**.) Daddy paid the deposit on our house but he knows we'll pay him back.

Sunita Doesn't your wife mind you coming back to London all the time?

Maurice Janice passed away. Seven years ago now. She had a tumour on the brain. We thought she'd had a stroke, but it turns out it was cancer. It was quick, in the end.

Harleen Oh no, we're so sorry, (*glaring at* **Sunita**) aren't we, Sunita?

Maurice Yeah. It was a hard time.

Sunita Yeah. Sorry.

Maurice Thank you.

Sunita Did you know, Mum? Maurice's wife died.

Harleen Seven years ago. From the big C.

Tejpal Yes, Maurice already told me.

Beat.

Nav You got kids?

Maurice No.

Nav You didn't want a family?

Harleen Not everyone wants kids, Nav.

Maurice It didn't happen for us.

Nav Right.

Maurice What about you two?

Nav We . . .

Harleen We're concentrating on our careers at the moment aren't we, Nav?

Beat. **Harleen** *and* **Nav** *glare at each other.*

Maurice So, you work for O2 don't you, Nav?

Nav Yeah.

Harleen He got promoted, four months ago, didn't you?

Nav Yeah.

Harleen He's Area Manager now.

Maurice Great.

Harleen Mum gets an upgrade whenever she wants one, doesn't she, Nav?

Nav Harleen, I keep telling you, you're on a two-year fixed contract. You went and signed that without asking me and now you're stuck with it. What part of that don't you get?

Harleen (*playing with* **Tejpal**'*s phone*) I really like this phone.

Nav (*relenting*) I tell you what. When I get my upgrade, I'll give you my new phone.

Harleen Really?

Nav And I'll wait for your upgrade.

Harleen By then there'll be a new phone. You'll probably give it to, Mum.

Maurice There's nothing wrong with a son looking out for his old mum is there?

Tejpal Not so much of the old please, Maurice.

Maurice *holds his hands up in apology to* **Tejpal** . . . *they share a laugh.* **Nav** *and* **Harleen** *share a look.*

Maurice So how long you two been together?

Nav We've been married nine years . . .

Harleen Ten years. Been together for nearly thirteen.

Nav We met at uni.

Harleen At the Sikh society disco.

Nav She was pissed!

Harleen So were you!

Nav Only ever had one rule.

Harleen (*flirty*) Had to break it when you met me though, didn't you?

Nav Never date an 'apni kurri'.

Harleen That means . . .

Maurice Never date one of your own!

Harleen How did you know that?

Maurice Oh I'm not just a pretty face.

Maurice *winks . . . making* **Harleen** *giggle . . .*

Harleen He couldn't keep away from me, Maurice!

Nav That's what she likes to think.

Harleen Nav . . . You're so cute sometimes.

They have a little kiss and cuddle . . .

Sunita God, will you two pack it in! You're making me feel sick.

This makes **Maurice** *laugh.*

Tejpal I hope you're all hungry!

Maurice Can't wait! What have we got?

Tejpal Rice, dhal, salad . . . mater paneer.

Maurice Roti?

Tejpal Of course roti! But I had to use ready-made.

Harleen We couldn't get the cooker to work.

Maurice So you said, Harleen.

Sunita We can't eat yet.

Nav Man! I'm starving!

Sunita We have to wait for Dad!

Tejpal Everything is ready. I don't want it getting cold.

Maurice Oh, is he coming? Your dad? He lives out in India now doesn't he?

Sunita No! He's just out there working.

Nav India's full of business opportunities.

Harleen Nav says India's the next superpower.

Maurice Maybe. If you've got money, you're all right, same as anywhere else. But most people are still held back by class and caste aren't they? Nobody's equal. Or maybe, some people make sure they stay more equal than others.

Tejpal *puts the roti on the table.*

Nav Mum! You haven't buttered the roti.

Tejpal No, I don't use butter anymore.

Nav Why not?

Tejpal It's better for you isn't it.

Harleen Mum's into olive oil now, aren't you, Mum?

Nav It won't taste the same, will it?

Tejpal Nav, I've been using olive oil for the last six months. Have you noticed any difference? You eat roti here every day.

Harleen I knew it!

Nav Mum!

Harleen I work all day . . .

Nav All right, Harleen . . .

Harleen It's not all right! You know I'm putting in extra hours because I'm trying to launch my own collection. I come home and spend ages cooking something nice for our dinner. I sit around waiting for him because I want us to eat together and when he finally waltzes in, he says 'oh, I'm not hungry'. And now I know why. It's because you're round here, stuffing yourself with Mum's aloo paratha and aloo gobi and saag bloody aloo! No wonder your jeans are too tight.

Nav I never asked you to cook for me!

Harleen I'm your wife! I can cook for you if I want to! You can't stop me!

Nav I wish I could stop you. I hate everything you cook Harleen! Full stop!

Harleen (*shocked*) What about my quinoa keema with pomegranate?

Nav Especially your bloody quinoa keema and pomegranate!

Harleen You said it was your favourite.

Nav I lied! It looks like pebble-dashed dog sick and it tastes like pebble-dashed dog sick!

Harleen Oh . . . you bloody two-faced, lying little . . .

Tejpal NAV! HARLEEN! Can we eat now?

Silence as they glare at each other.

They go to the table.

Harleen *makes a face as she takes lids off bowls and sniffs each dish.*

Tejpal *puts food on a plate and gives it to* **Maurice**.

Nav Mum, where's the chicken?

Tejpal I didn't make chicken.

Nav We always have chicken!

Tejpal The Baba said we shouldn't eat meat on Fridays.

Nav What? Laddoo baba?

Tejpal Yes.

Nav Anyone can go around saying he's a guru. That's how they rake in the money.

Harleen Did you use olive oil for this, Mum?

Tejpal YES, Harleen, YES!! I used olive oil for this! How many times do I have to tell you? Now stop fussing and eat!

Harleen (*tearful*) I'm not making a fuss. I can't help it if I've got allergies. Intolerances . . . (*Punjabi*) I blow up!

Tejpal Sit and eat. Harleen shall I put some on for you?

Harleen (*sulky*) I'll help myself.

Tejpal Sunita?

Sunita (*rudely*) Ke?

Tejpal Come and eat.

Sunita Not yet!

Tejpal Come on. We're celebrating your birthday. Come and eat with us, Sunita.

Maurice Lovely jubbly!

Harleen *and* **Nav** *clock this.*

Harleen I suppose I'll have to have the salad. (*To* **Maurice**.) This is dhal.

Maurice I know, Harleen. I've had it before. And Tej made some for me.

Nav Did she.

Maurice Nothing like a home-cooked dhal. No butter though. She used olive oil cos I try not to eat butter. Got to keep tabs on the cholesterol.

Beat.

Nav (*passing the dhal over to* **Harleen**) Here you go . . . yeah, so . . . made with *olive oil* so Harleen will love that. You know, she actually thought it was because of *her* Mum didn't use . . . /

Harleen *nudges* **Nav** *hard.*

Nav Ouch!

Beat.

Harleen (*Punjabi*) I don't eat dhal.

Silence as they start to eat. **Sunita** *comes over.*

Sunita You're still here.

Harleen (*trying to deflect*) So, I left work early, Maurice, just so I could be here. We've got a big showcase this evening. Do you know Gok Wan?

Maurice I know of him.

Harleen I work for someone who knows him.

Sunita Why are you still here?

Maurice Your mum invited me to your birthday party.

Sunita I didn't even want a party.

Nav I told you.

Harleen Mum got you an eggless cake.

Nav And we're not even vegetarians.

Sunita Which you forgot to pick up because you're too busy with your fancy fashion showcase.

Harleen I didn't forget actually. I didn't know I had to collect your stupid cake because he didn't tell me.

Nav All right! All right!! I forgot to tell you. Can we leave it now?!

Sunita (*to* **Maurice**) She had no right to invite you.

Tejpal Sunita . . .

Sunita It's up to me who comes to my party.

Tejpal Sunita, stop it, please.

Sunita So you can go!

Maurice You're behaving like a spoiled brat.

Sunita (*outraged*) Who do you think you are? My dad?

Maurice (*gentle*) No Sunita. I'm not your dad. So don't take your shit out on me.

Nav (*standing*) Mate, no one talks to my sister like that!

Maurice (*calmly*) I don't have to put up with her moods and tantrums.

Sunita I don't have moods and tantrums.

Maurice She's behaving like a five-year-old.

Nav That's just how she is.

Sunita (*to* **Nav**) Excuse me?

Maurice I find it hard to keep my mouth shut when someone around me is being rude. Especially when your mum's gone to a lot of trouble.

Sunita How dare you . . .

Maurice Everyone is trying to make an effort.

Sunita Are they? Well, that makes a change! Usually they just like to talk about me . . .

Maurice Your mum's cooked your favourite dishes. She got you a cake. Your brother's here . . .

Harleen And me. I left work early. I'm supposed to be at a showcase.

Maurice (*gentle*) It's not their fault your dad isn't here, Sunita, so don't take it out on them.

Nav (*protective*) It's ok. It's ok. We don't need to . . .

Harleen It's not ok. Maurice is right.

Sunita My dad's busy. He's running his business in India. You know nothing about it.

Maurice I know he's getting on with his life.

Harleen That's what I said.

Nav Shut up, Harleen.

Harleen Don't tell me to shut up.

Maurice What are you doing with yours? What are you waiting around for?

Sunita He's coming home.

Maurice Is he?

Sunita Get out!

Maurice He left. No explanations.

Sunita Get out!!

Maurice No apologies.

Sunita Get out! Get out!!

Maurice When was the last time he rang you?

Nav (*getting angrier*) Now listen, mate . . .

Harleen Nav, calm down.

Sunita He's coming home. I know he is.

Maurice Well you just keep telling yourself that.

Sunita HE'S COMING HOME! He has to!

Sunita *breaks down.* **Tejpal** *takes her in her arms and comforts her . . .*

Tejpal Sunita . . . Sunita . . . Please . . . (*Punjabi*) Enough. Enough . . . .

Harleen *gets a glass of water for* **Sunita** *and tries to fuss over her . . . Plumping up cushions around her and stroking her hair, tissues etc.* **Sunita** *eventually calms down although she is still very upset.*

Nav (*to* **Maurice**) You've got no right upsetting her like this.

Maurice Isn't it time she faced the truth? Isn't it time you all did?

Nav Who the hell are you? Bloody Yoda?

Maurice How long can you keep pretending? Life's too short mate. You all need to move on. Your father has.

Nav (*simmering anger*) I think you'd better leave.

Maurice He walked out on you and you've spent the last twenty years pretending he's just popped out for a pint of milk.

Nav I don't want you here.

Tejpal Nav.

Nav (*accusing*) You cooked dhal for him?

Tejpal Shut up and sit down!

Nav *sits down. Silence.*

The Guru Nanak picture twinkles gently in the background.

Tejpal We are going to celebrate Sunita's birthday.

Tejpal *takes a bottle a bottle of prosecco from the fridge.* **Nav** *goes to take it off her.*

Tejpal Sit down.

Nav *sits down, fidgeting with his turban.*

Tejpal Maurice. Please.

She gives the bottle to **Maurice** *to open. He pours everyone a glass.*

Beat. Awkward.

All Cheers!

Maurice Life begins when you're ready, Sunita!

They all drink.

Sunita (*tearful*) Mum . . .

Harleen What's wrong with her now?

Nav Mid-life crisis, innit?

Tejpal *takes* **Sunita** *in her arms.*

Harleen Don't just stand there!

Nav What do you want me to do?

Harleen Make her feel better.

Nav It's a bit late for that.

Sunita He should've have been here.

Harleen He who?

Sunita I really thought he'd come.

Tejpal I know.

Harleen (*surprised*) Have you got a boyfriend?

Nav She thought you were a lesbian.

Harleen It doesn't matter if you are.

Sunita I'm not.

Harleen It's ok to be gay.

Sunita I'm not gay.

Harleen Or Bi.

Sunita I'm not lesbian, gay, binary . . .

Harleen It's non-binary . . .

Sunita (*accusing* **Nav**) God! You know nothing about me! Just because I don't overshare like some people (*pointedly at* **Harleen**) doesn't mean I haven't had friends or a boyfriend.

Nav You're right! And whose fault is that? How am I supposed to know anything about you? Or what's going on in your life if you don't *talk* to me? You're my sister!

Sunita You didn't want me around. Not after you met *her*.

Nav That's not true and you know it. So don't blame Harleen. It's you! You're the one always pushing us away. Always making us feel bad. I don't even know what I'm supposed to have done to upset you.

Sunita I DON'T KNOW EITHER!!

Beat.

I just . . . It's me. My life . . . I'm waiting and waiting and I don't know what for!

Maurice You're waiting for your dad, Sunita.

Silence . . . as the truth of this hangs in the air . . .

Sunita I really thought he'd be here today you know? I just wanted to hold his hand. I wanted it to be like it was, when we were little. I thought he'd remember my birthday.

Beat.

But he doesn't want anything to do with us, does he?

Tejpal No. He doesn't.

Sunita Why? What did I do?

Tejpal You didn't do anything, Sunita. You have to believe that.

Sunita I tried calling him. He never picks up.

Tejpal When?

Sunita Today. All week. And . . . and . . . I sent him a ticket. I thought if I sent him the ticket, he'd have to come. But he didn't.

Tejpal But . . .

Sunita I rang Minder Chacha (*uncle*).

Tejpal I haven't spoken to him since your dad left.

Sunita I told him we had to send some legal stuff, that I needed his correct address. His phone number's still the same you know. He just didn't want to speak to me. That's why he never answered his phone.

Beat.

Nav Dad's not coming back, Sunita.

Sunita I know. We've always known, haven't we?

Nav Yeah.

Sunita Then why didn't we ever talk about it?!!

Harleen That's what I said.

Nav We should've.

Tejpal I didn't know what to say. How to say it.

Nav It was easier to pretend.

Sunita I don't understand why he didn't want us. I keep thinking, over and over. What did I do wrong? What did you say to make him go away?

Tejpal I didn't say anything. I promise.

Sunita I know that now. It was him. And all this time . . . we've been pretending. Hiding.

Nav It was just easier that way, sis.

Sunita Was it? Do you really believe that?

Silence.

Maurice *goes and stands with* **Tejpal**.

Maurice Tej?

Nav Tej?

Maurice We should . . .

Tejpal Yes, Maurice.

Maurice *puts his arm round* **Tejpal**.

Nav Take your hands off my mother.

Harleen Oh my god!! Are you . . .? You and him . . .?

Maurice We've become friends, haven't we?

Tejpal Good friends.

Sunita Are you serious?! It's my birthday!

Harleen So that's why the kitchen took so long!

Maurice I've invited your mum out to Spain.

Tejpal For a holiday. I'm going on holiday. With Maurice.

Nav You're not going anywhere.

Tejpal Just listen to me.

Nav Tell him to leave, Mum.

Tejpal I don't want to Nav.

Nav (*outraged*) What do you think you're doing? You can't just run off with another bloke like some love-struck sixteen-year-old. You're nearly sixty!

Tejpal I'm fifty-seven.

Nav It's disgusting.

Tejpal If I wanted to run off, I'd have left without telling any of you. Just packed my bags and gone.

Sunita Gone? Gone where?

Nav And what do you think people are going to say when they find out?

Tejpal I don't care what people say anymore. Let them say what they want. What's new? They've been talking behind my back since your father left. Did anyone come and ask me if *I* was ok? Knock on the door and see if we needed anything? No! Too busy laughing at me and whispering about my bad kismet. Knowing I couldn't say anything. What was there to say?

Maurice The truth? Sometimes, facing it makes you stronger.

Nav (*furious*) Fucking Yoda speaks again!!!

Nav *goes to punch* **Maurice**, **Harleen** *stops him.*

Harleen No! Stop it, Nav.

Angry silence.

You and Maurice . . . when . . . how did all this happen?

Tejpal I don't know. Slowly. We talked. And laughed and for the first time I felt . . . (*She takes his hand.*) Everyone knows your father has another woman. He's married to me, but he wants to be with her. Maurice is right. It's time we faced the truth. How long do we keep living like this? You said yourself, Sunita . . . Pretending? Where has it got us? Your father's made a new life for himself. It's time we did the same.

Nav A new life? With him?

Tejpal Maybe. Yes.

Harleen Listen to me, Mum, when he's taken all your money, he'll dump you and move onto someone else. That's what men like him do. He's taking advantage of you because you're old and vulnerable!

Tejpal No, Harleen! I'm not old. Not yet. Yes, I was vulnerable . . . when their father left me to bring up two children on my own, when the ladies at the gurdwara whispered about his woman back in India. Every time Sunita asked me when Dad was coming home, I felt vulnerable. But not any more, Harleen. Not now. Not ever again.

Nav You know nothing about him.

Tejpal I know enough.

Harleen But he doesn't speak Punjabi!

Tejpal Neither do you!

Beat.

Harleen They say women going through the change go through a horny stage . . .

Nav You're just putting dirty thoughts in my head.

Harleen It's obviously true!

Nav Nobody should be thinking of *that* at your age!!

Maurice Listen, son! Your mother is a beautiful woman. She's intelligent. Funny. Strong. And she's been through a lot.

Nav Feeling sorry for the little Indian woman? Is that your thing? Go and do your charity work somewhere else, mate, we don't need it here!

Maurice What are you getting all heated about? Don't you want your mum to be happy?

Nav She doesn't fit in your world, mate. My mum's never even been to a pub, how do you think she'll feel when you start dragging her out for fancy cocktails in Marbella?

Maurice Why don't you ask her?

Nav (*to* **Tejpal**) You've been out for a drink with him?

Tejpal The president of the golf club is Sikh actually. And his wife is very nice too.

Maurice Seems to me, you're the one who sees her as the 'little Indian Woman', mate, not me.

Nav *punches* **Maurice**. *They fight.*

Tejpal Stop it!

Harleen Pack it in, Nav!

Harleen *and* **Tejpal** *manage to pull them apart.* **Nav**'*s turban comes off during the fight. We see his trendy haircut . . . Silence.*

Nav *is shame-faced. He can't look his mother in the eye.* **Harleen** *picks up his turban and holds it.*

Tejpal All this time and you think I didn't know?

Exit **Nav**.

Tejpal You watched him cut his hair and didn't say anything?

Harleen (*babbling*) I wasn't there . . . honest. He wanted to tell you. But he didn't know how to . . . he was so scared. He knew you'd be upset. So he thought if he didn't say anything, his hair would grow back, eventually, and you didn't need to ever find out, because . . .

Enter **Nav** *with a small package.*

Nav Shut up, Harleen. Just. Shut. Up.

He gives the package to **Tejpal**. *She opens the package. It is his hair.*

Harleen We don't have any secrets in my family.

Nav Yeah, Harleen . . . we know. You're better than us.

Harleen I didn't say that.

Nav Why do you think I cut my hair, Harleen?

Harleen I don't know do I?

Nav I didn't want to cut my hair. But I did it for you.

Harleen For me?

Nav I know it's what's in here (*indicating his heart*) that's important, not how you look. My turban, my hair, it didn't make me a better Sikh. But it's a part of who I am. The day I cut my hair, I cut away a part of me. For you!

Harleen How many times have you walked around in a beanie or your hair in a ponytail?

Nav This, this, this (*indicating his shoes, clothes, hair*) all for you.

Harleen There's nothing wrong with being hip and modern.

Nav I did it because I love you.

Harleen I love you too but it's got nothing to do with it.

Nav I did it for you, Harleen!

Harleen Why are you making me feel bad?

Nav What have you ever done for me?

Harleen Are you actually being serious?

Nav We go round to your posh parents, in your posh car, drinking posh organic wine.

Harleen I resent that.

Nav Eating Parmesan cheese crisps.

Sunita Cheese cheese crisps?

Harleen (*to* **Sunita**) You shut up. (*To* **Nav**.) Don't bring my parents into this.

Nav You can't give me one small thing?

Harleen I gave you marriage. What more do you want?

Nav I WANT BABIES!!!

Harleen The night before we got married, I drove around for miles and miles. Part of me wanted to run away. I nearly did. But I didn't want to lose you. I couldn't imagine living without you. Because I love you so much. So I came home and the next day, we got married. And I'm glad. I'm so glad. But you know, Nav, a lot of women make decisions just to keep other people happy. Parents. Husbands. The in-laws.

Children. (*Looking at* **Tejpal**.) The bloody community. I'm not that kind of woman. You've always known that. And you've always known I didn't want babies.

Nav If we don't have children, Harleen, it will break my heart.

Harleen You cut your hair because you didn't fit in with your friends, and now, you don't fit in with your friends because you don't have babies!

Nav *and* **Harleen** *stare at each other.*

Tejpal I used to comb your hair every night, do you remember?

Nav Yeah.

Tejpal (*to* **Maurice**) He had such beautiful hair.

Beat.

When I was young, we didn't have any choices. We didn't dare go against our parents' wishes. Nobody *asked* if you were in love. If you were lucky, you fell in love with the man you married and he fell in love with you. How often that happened, I don't know. But one thing I do know, marriage isn't easy, (*to* **Harleen**) even when you marry the man you love. Your father isn't a bad man. Our parents arranged our marriage, so we got married. It was our duty. But he didn't want to be with me. He was never in love with me.

Sunita He told you that?

Tejpal I realized very quickly he was in love with someone else and always had been.

Sunita The woman in India?

Tejpal He didn't want to be with me.

Nav He should've told you the truth.

Tejpal I know.

Nav So he just abandoned us?

Sunita He had responsibilities! I can't believe he just . . . I always thought my dad was . . . was a . . . but he's just a coward isn't he?

Tejpal He's just a man, Sunita. Maybe he was scared too.

Silence.

Nav What about us?

Tejpal You're a grown man, Nav. You have a beautiful wife who loves you. Live your life! Be happy.

Sunita All this time you've been carrying on with him, behind our backs.

Tejpal No, Sunita, I've done nothing wrong. I've spent my life running around after you two and now you don't need me anymore. Stand on your own two feet.

Sunita We do need you. *I* need you.

Tejpal What do you want me to do? Cook your dinner, wash your clothes and watch my life fade away? Grow old, quietly? I won't! I want to live my life, what's left of it. Now it's time for me. I'm going to Spain, with Maurice. So just deal with it, ok?

Sunita So that's it, is it? You're going to sail off into the Spanish sunset, happy to wash *his* smelly socks and pants? Doesn't matter what we think or what we want. Now suddenly it's all about following *your* heart? Well what about me? What am I supposed to do now?

Tejpal What do you want to do, Sunita?

Sunita I DON'T KNOW! I wanted to go to university once. *You* wouldn't let me.

Tejpal That was wrong of me.

Sunita I begged you to let me go.

Tejpal I should've supported you.

Sunita I could've have done something with my life!

Tejpal I know. I'm sorry. I don't know what else to say.

Sunita I should've just fucked off. Like my dad. Gone to uni and told you to *just deal with it*! But I was never that brave.

Tejpal And neither was I. I didn't know how to follow my dreams, Sunita. People always think a woman who thinks for herself, who speaks her mind is dangerous. So I didn't talk about my dreams or what was in my heart. And I was scared. Scared to let you follow your dreams. I didn't know how to. But keeping quiet didn't make my life better. It just made it lonely. Then I met Maurice . . . and I know you think I've gone mad, maybe I have . . . but when I met Maurice, I met a man who listens to me, who makes me laugh, who makes me feel like I matter and that I have a place in this world. So for the first time in my life . . . I *am* going to be brave. I *am* going to follow my heart. And I don't care what anyone thinks. And, I want you to do the same.

Tejpal *takes* **Sunita***'s face in her hands, she kisses her.*

Tejpal I love you so much. And I am so so sorry I didn't let you be you. Be you now, ok?

Sunita *nods.*

Tejpal Promise me.

Sunita I'll try.

Tejpal No. Promise me.

Sunita Promise.

Tejpal I love you.

Sunita I love you too.

They hug.

Maurice Tej?

Tejpal Yes, we need to go.

Nav You're going now?

Harleen Tonight? We haven't done the cake yet!

Tejpal Come on, let's do it now. We have to go, we have a very early flight tomorrow.

Maurice I've booked us into the Sheraton tonight.

Awkward silence as they process this . . . **Tejpal** *is flustered,* **Sunita** *takes her hands, looks her in the eyes, and calms her down.*

Sunita Mum, go.

Harleen What about all your stuff?

Tejpal I'm going on holiday, Harleen, not emigrating.

Harleen But are you going to move to Spain?

Tejpal Let's see what happens, henna Maurice?

Maurice Let's take one step at a time, Tej. It's all we can do.

Tejpal (*nodding*) Only Waheguru knows.

Beat.

This is something I have to do. I know you might not agree but I hope one day, you'll understand.

Nav *goes to* **Maurice**, *tense.*

Nav I don't know what you think you're doing, and I don't know what makes you think you can just walk in here and take our mum away from us . . .

Maurice Not take away, mate. Love. Cherish. If she'll let me.

Harleen*'s heart melts . . .* **Nav** *and* **Maurice** *eyeball each other . . . but then,* **Nav** *shakes* **Maurice***'s hand.*

Nav Take care of her, man . . .

Maurice Always. I promise.

Tejpal *hugs them. Then goes to the Guru Nanak picture and says a quick prayer.*

Tejpal Chullo, Maurice. I'll WhatsApp you in the morning.

Exit **Maurice** *and* **Tejpal**.

Silence.

Harleen *pours herself a glass of prosecco, pulls a bowl of crisps towards her and eats.*

Nav (*teasing, in Punjabi*) I don't eat crisps.

Nav *manages to make* **Harleen** *laugh. They have a tentative smile . . .*

Harleen Are we ok?

Nav Come on you. Let's get you home.

An unsteady **Harleen** *collects her bags. She picks up the remaining prosecco bottles.*

She finds her present for **Sunita** *and tentatively sidles up to her, holding out the present.*

Harleen I hope you like the present. I designed it myself.

Sunita Thank you.

Harleen *turns to go.*

Sunita Harleen?

It's not true. What I said before.

Beat.

You're alright.

They smile. **Harleen** *gives* **Sunita** *a hug.*

Harleen (*gently*) Happy Birthday, Sunita. Don't forget to do the cake. And make sure you make a wish.

As **Harleen** *exits.*

Harleen Nav? You coming or what?

Sunita (*to* **Nav**) Hold on!

Sunita *takes the last bottle from the fridge and hands it to* **Nav**. *He turns to leave but changing his mind, he gives the bottle back to* **Sunita**.

Nav Treat yourself, sis. You deserve it.

Sunita Yeah.

Beat.

Nav Funny birthday.

Sunita One to remember innit.

Nav Yeah.

Sunita Yeah.

Beat. **Nav** *turns to leave.*

Sunita I might go university. Do you think it's too late? Am I being stupid?

Nav No. You've always been the smart one in this family. If you don't apply, I'm gonna do it for you.

They smile at each other. **Nav** *picks up his turban and turns to leave.*

Sunita Maybe we can go to the cinema on Wednesday. (*Unsure.*)

If you'd like?

Nav (*shouting back*) I'd like. Happy Birthday, sis. Love ya.

Exit **Nav**.

Sunita *looks around the room.*

She picks up the present left by **Harleen**, *gives it a squeeze, holds it to her ear, squeezing it. She opens it and puts the scarf around her neck.*

She walks to the table and surveys the half-eaten birthday dinner. She opens her card and finds £101. She places the card on the table and pockets the money.

She pulls the cake towards her, looks at it for a moment and lights the candle. She sings . . .

Sunita Happy Birthday to me. Happy Birthday to me. Happy Birthday to Sunita. Happy Birthday to me!

She takes a deep breath and makes a wish. **Sunita** *blows out the candle.*

Suddenly, her phone rings. She watches the screen as it rings and rings. She ignores the call, letting it click to voicemail.

We hear the beep and message (please leave a message after the tone) it's her dad . . .

Dad Hello? Sunita? It's your daddy here . . .

She abruptly hangs up, throwing her phone onto the sofa.

Sunita *stands quietly for a moment, taking in the room. The picture of Guru Nanak twinkles gently above her.*

Slowly **Sunita** *allows herself a smile . . . there are healing tears rolling down her face.*

She takes off the cardigan, folds it gently and places it down. She opens the prosecco bottle with a loud pop and drinks.

'Happy Birthday Sunita' (Mohd. Rafi) begins . . .

Exit **Sunita**, *with prosecco bottle in hand . . . Lights fade as music plays out.*

The End.

Printed in the USA
CPSIA information can be obtained
at www.ICGtesting.com
LVHW011739161223
766614LV00004B/206